AF604881

THE SMALLEST FROG IN THE WORLD

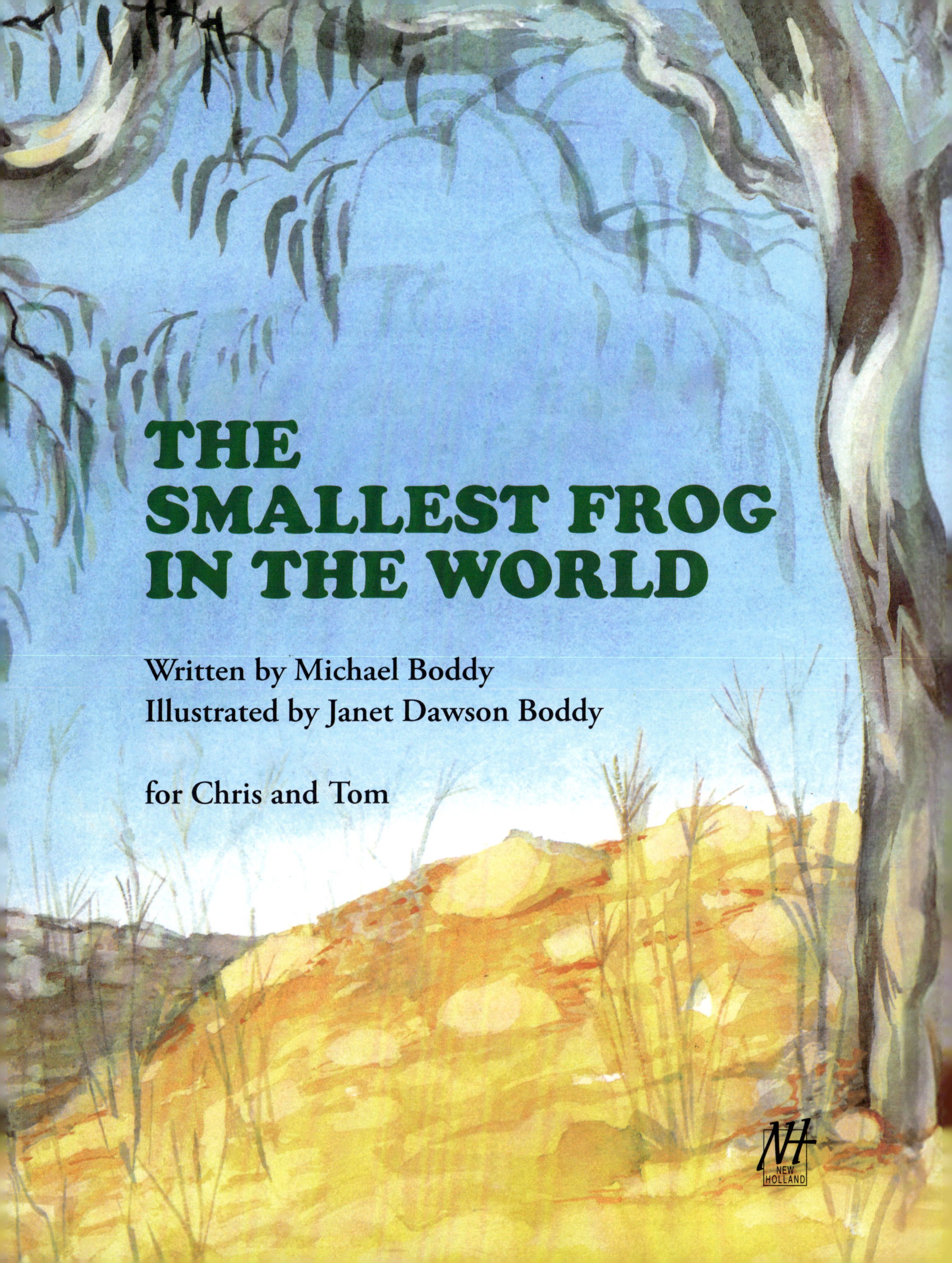

THE SMALLEST FROG IN THE WORLD

Written by Michael Boddy
Illustrated by Janet Dawson Boddy

for Chris and Tom

NEW HOLLAND

It was so dry. There had been no rain for months. Everything was withering under the hot sun.

The Smallest Frog in the World sat under a stone by the creek. It was really a little cave and it kept him from drying up. It also kept him well hidden from the old Brown Snake who came down every day to this spot for a drink.

''It's not a good life for a frog,'' the Smallest Frog said to himself, ''when there's hardly any water in the creek. I wish it would rain!''

Far away, a cloud started to grow. It got bigger and bigger and blacker and blacker. It rumbled as it grew and with every rumble it let out huge drops of rain.

It was a big thunder-cloud. Any minute there was going to be a storm.

What a storm! Wind, water, claps of thunder, lightning! a monster of a storm!

Two hares on the hillside tried to find a place to hide. They shivered as the cold wind blew and the rain pelted down. But they were pleased at the same time. The water would help the grass to grow. Soon they would have juicy green shoots to eat.

The rain came down very fast. In fact, there was so much rain that a lot of it ran off the ground straight into the creek without soaking into the ground at all.

After the rain had gone, the Smallest Frog in the World left his cave to see the water. WHOOSH! A mass of water rushed down the creek and carried him away with it. He found it hard to swim, the water was gushing so fast.

The gushing water carried the Smallest Frog far away down the creek. He struggled and struggled until at last he managed to reach the bank and hold on to a Cumbungi reed that was growing there.

He clung to the Cumbungi reed for ages. Finally he found enough strength to pull himself out of the water and up on to the bank.

He lay there exhausted. “Oh well,” he said to himself, “I may be exhausted and far from home, but I *am* safe. I’ll stay here until the water goes down.”

The tired insects clinging to the reed-stems above him were thinking exactly the same thing!

KOK-KOK!
KIKIK
-BOK
KNEEDEEP!
KIK-KRRK!
KIK-KO
BONK!
BRRK!
BOK!
KEK KEK!
BAGGERLAGS!

That night the water went down. It was a wet, warm night and every frog in the district came out to have fun. There were some that the Smallest Frog had never seen before. They sat half in and half out of the water amongst the reeds and started to sing.

What a noise! Each frog made its own sound – KOK KOK KOK! KNEE DEEP! BAGGERLAGS! BUGUNCLE! BONK!

BOK! KEK KEK KEK! BRRRK! Such a noise! Some of the animals that have to work hard at night stopped to listen.

The Smallest Frog in the World was still exhausted but he wanted to join in. He took a deep breath and inflated the air-sac under his chin. "UK UK UK UK UK!" he called in his tiny voice.

No one heard him. They were too busy with their KNEE DEEP! KEK KEK KEK KEK! BRRRRK! KOK KOK KOK KOK! BAGGERLAGS! BONK! to take any notice of him. He felt very lonely.

He decided to go back to his own little cave. At least he would feel at home there.

The moon was very bright after the storm. He climbed up the bank of the creek and set off on his journey.

The next day he was lost. He didn't know where he was at all. It was hot and the sun burned his skin.

There was an old Crow sitting in a tree nearby. This frightened him a lot. Crows are not kind to little frogs. He hid under a leaf.

Luckily the Crow didn't spot him. It flew away calling "CAW CAW CAAAAAAAW!"

The Smallest Frog in the World looked round for another place to hide and saw something that nearly made his eyes pop out of his head. It was a beautiful green forest with waving trees and shady groves.

"It'll be damp and cool under those trees and in those groves," he thought. "I'll be able to hide there too, from crows and snakes." He hopped towards the green forest as quickly as he could.

The Smallest Frog was right. It was *very* cool and pleasant amongst the waving trees and damp shady groves!

"What a wonderful smell!" thought the Smallest Frog. "I've never seen trees and shrubs that smell so exciting!"

Funnily enough, no one was living there. Or so it seemed to him. He set out to explore.

There was a grand avenue of trees with thick red stumps and tall feathery branches.

"The sun won't burn my skin here," thought the Smallest Frog. "The feathery branches make such good shade." And he jumped for joy.

He found a fountain playing. It was splashing water all over some huge shrubs with crinkly dark-green leaves.

"My goodness!" he thought. "Shrubs as big as this to hide under! Better than a cave in a creek-bank!"

He danced under the fountain and felt cool again.

He found a tower reaching up into the sky. "I'll climb that tower," he thought, "and see what else is in this remarkable place."

He struggled and heaved and pushed and shoved ...

. . . until he reached the top of the tower. The forest was spread out beneath him.

He caught a passing fly. GLOP! "This is the life," he thought. But a Willy Wagtail flew down and around his head and shrieked at him: "Get down from there! These are *my* flies! I eat these! Go and find your own flies!" She batted at him with her wings and shrieked louder than before.

"How rude!" thought the Smallest Frog as he scrambled down the tower.

Soon he found a very exciting spot. There were large, twisty trees with a mysterious, tangy smell. From the branches of these mysterious, tangy trees there hung huge globes of green, yellow and shiny red.

He sat down to rest under the reddest cluster of globes and felt full of happiness."UK UK UK UK UK UK!" he shouted in as big a voice as he could. It sounded good amongst the tangy trees.

Just then he heard a noise. It was a pattering-scuffling growly-snuffling sort of noise.

"Help!" said the Smallest Frog to himself. "That noise sounds *big!*" He looked round for somewhere to hide. "Just while I see what it is," he added bravely.

Luckily, there was a cave quite close, next to the twisty, tangy trees with the huge coloured globes. He hid himself there as the scuffly-snuffly-growly-pattering creature came closer.

"I'II frighten this growly-snuffly thing," thought the Smallest Frog in the World. "I'll frighten it. Then it'll go away and leave me alone."

He took a deeeeeeeep breath and inflated his air-sac. "UK UK UK UK UK UK!" he shouted. Because he was inside the cave he sounded very loud indeed with all the echoes. "UK UK UK UK UK UK!"

And the echoes rang again.

The snuffly-growly creature wasn't frightened at all. It seemed to think the noise was very funny. With its nose it tipped over the cave.

The Smallest Frog in the World tumbled out of the cave. The snuffly-growly creature looked at him for a moment and laughed even more.

"Something as small as you making so much noise!" it said and laughed and laughed.

"How dare you!" said the Smallest Frog. "You can't come along here and do what you like. This place is mine! I'm the boss here!"

"Wait till Big Mike hears that," said the snuffly-growly creature. "He'll laugh too!"

"Big Mike? What's a Big Mike?" asked the Smallest Frog.

Before the snuffly-growly creature could reply a huge rumbling voice said: "What's all the noise about?"

An enormous animal clumped into view. The Smallest Frog turned pale green with fright. At last he dared to look up and see what sort of animal it was. He had to look up and up because it was so tall. He saw a red cloud high up in the air at the very top.

"It's a sort of walking tree with a thunderstorm on top," thought the Smallest Frog. "That's why it rumbles when it talks."

The voice rumbled out of the red cloud: "What's all the noise about, Lulu?"

"Ho Ho!" said the snuffly-growly creature whose name was Lulu. "Wait till you hear."

The walking tree swayed about and the rumbling voice said: "Well well well! What have you got there, Lulu? It must be a frog from the creek. The smallest frog in the world from what I can see."

The Smallest Frog jumped onto the foot of the walking tree. He was very cross and forgot how frightened he was.

"I bet you I'm *not* the smallest frog in the world," he said. "In fact I'm a Spotted Grass Frog and my proper name is *Limnodynastes tasmaniensis."*

"What a mouthful!" rumbled the voice. The walking tree shook with laughter. "I wouldn't like a name like that!"

"I don't like it much either," said the Smallest Frog. "But it's a better name than some I've heard!"

"Like mine for instance?" rumbled the walking tree.

"I don't care what you're called," said the Smallest Frog. "Just remember I found this place first. It's all mine. I don't care how much you laugh at me or how big you are. I saw it first!"

"That's what *you* think, *Limnodynastes whatchermercallit,"* said the rumbling voice with a chuckle.

The Smallest Frog was about to say: *"Tasmaniensis! If* you don't mind!", and blow himself up to double his size to show how tough he was. But he was picked up instead and whisked into the air, far off the ground to the top of the walking tree. He could see a huge pair of blue eyes, a nose and a mouth. The red thunder-cloud was really a big fluffy red beard.

"Gosh!" he gasped. "I've seen creatures like you down at the creek. You're just a big *person* aren't you?"

"My name is Michael," said the big person.

"Big Mike," said Lulu.

"I thought you were a walking tree," said the Smallest Frog.

Michael and Lulu roared with laughter. Michael laughed so hard he nearly blew the Smallest Frog off his finger.

"I'm a gardener," said Michael. "This place is a garden where we grow vegetables and flowers for people. I live here with my wife Janet and my dog Lulu. There are lots of other creatures living here too. We all work in the garden."

The Smallest Frog looked round nervously. He *was* very far off the ground.

"I can't see anyone else," he said in a very small voice. "Except for that snuffly-growly *dog* creature called Lulu who keeps laughing at me. I thought there was just me and that it was my garden."

"Then it's time you woke up, Little Frog," said Michael, in his big rumbly voice.

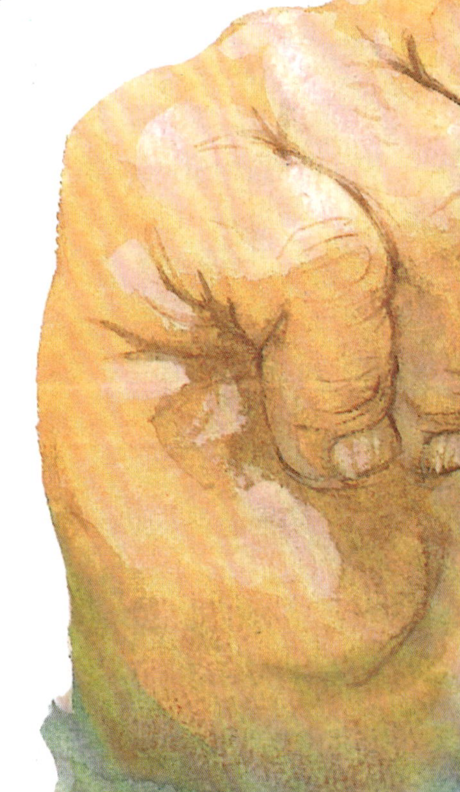

"This garden is full of creatures, big and small," Michael went on. "If you keep your eyes and ears open you will see that each one has an important job to do."

"They don't *look* very important," said the Smallest Frog. 'For a start, they can't catch flies as well as I can."

"That's what you think!" shrieked the Willy Wagtail, who had been listening. "And I can *fly* as well. You can't do that!"

"What about me?" said the Garden Spider. "I catch all sorts of insects. You can't build a web as good as this!"

"Well I guard the gate and bark when there's danger," said Lulu. "I'd like to see you doing that!"

"And I do the digging and weeding," said Michael. "I'd like to see you doing that!"

" And I draw pictures of the plants and flowers so that people will get to know them better," said Michael's wife Janet, popping out from behind a tree with pencil and paper in hand. "I'd like to see you doing *that!'*

"Oh dear!" said the Smallest Frog. "I've said all the wrong things!"

"Of course you have!" said a Praying Mantis on a leaf. "We all work very hard here, you know, eating caterpillars and earwigs and vegetable bugs that want to spoil the vegetables and flowers in this garden."

"Here here!" said a small Gekko who was clinging upside down on the fence. "I'm as good a fly-catcher as you, Little Frog. And I walk upside-down and change colour whenever I feel like it. I'd like to see you doing that!"

"I'm sorry," said the Smallest Frog. "I've really made a fool of myself."

"Give credit where credit's due!" shouted a Honeybee, buzzing busily past.

"Look at that Honeybee," said Michael. "It pollinates the flowers."

"*And* I make honey which goes very well on hot buttered toast," said the Honeybee. "But I'm too busy to talk about it at the moment."

"You're not too busy – you're too *buzzy*!" said Lulu. She thought that was a very good joke.

"I'll sting your nose, you cheeky dog!" said the Honeybee, buzzing a lot.

"Now then! Now then!" said Michael. "We must all stay friends." And he carefully put the Smallest Frog back down on the ground.

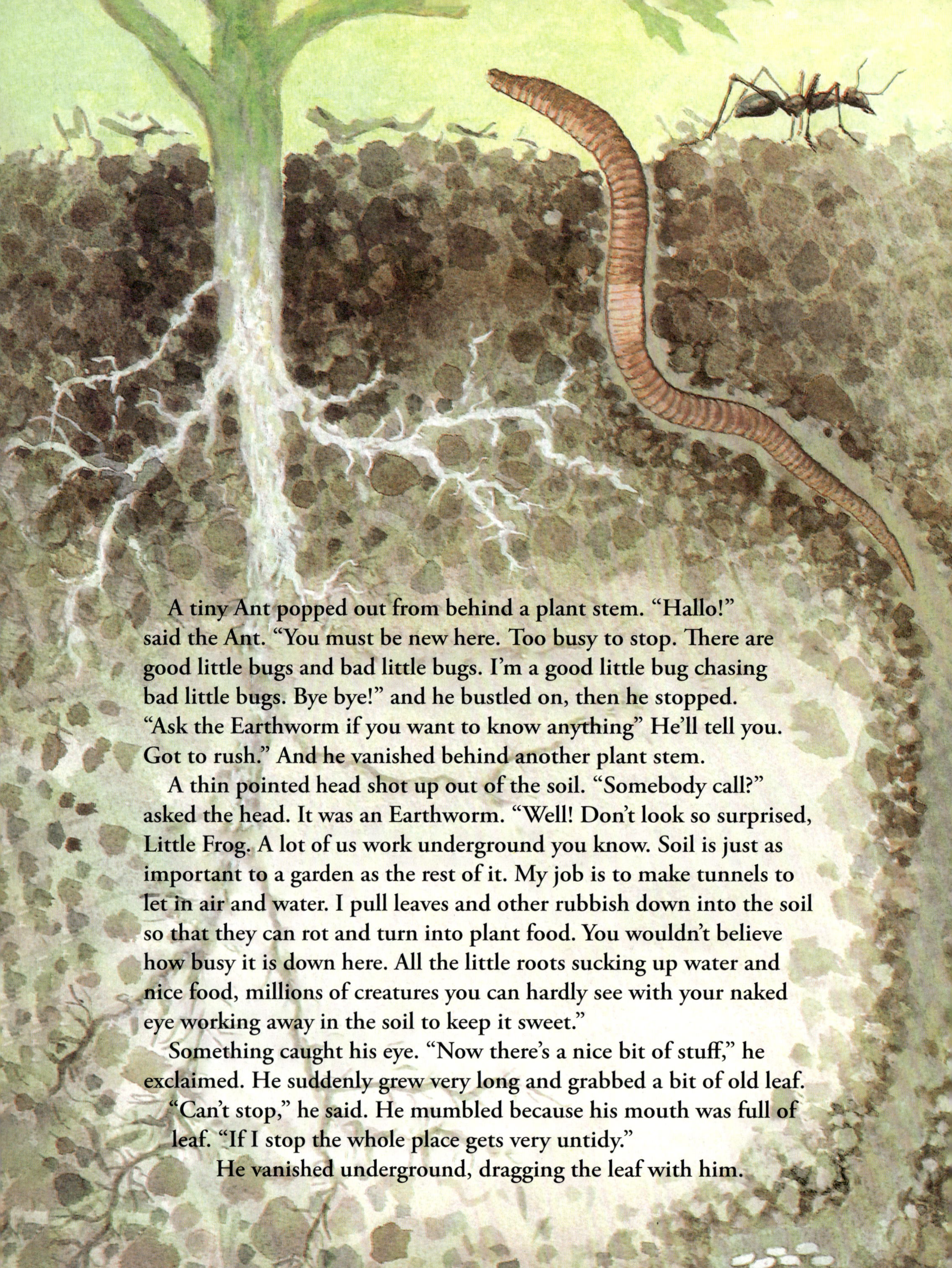

A tiny Ant popped out from behind a plant stem. “Hallo!” said the Ant. “You must be new here. Too busy to stop. There are good little bugs and bad little bugs. I’m a good little bug chasing bad little bugs. Bye bye!” and he bustled on, then he stopped. “Ask the Earthworm if you want to know anything” He’ll tell you. Got to rush.” And he vanished behind another plant stem.

A thin pointed head shot up out of the soil. “Somebody call?” asked the head. It was an Earthworm. “Well! Don’t look so surprised, Little Frog. A lot of us work underground you know. Soil is just as important to a garden as the rest of it. My job is to make tunnels to let in air and water. I pull leaves and other rubbish down into the soil so that they can rot and turn into plant food. You wouldn’t believe how busy it is down here. All the little roots sucking up water and nice food, millions of creatures you can hardly see with your naked eye working away in the soil to keep it sweet.”

Something caught his eye. “Now there’s a nice bit of stuff,” he exclaimed. He suddenly grew very long and grabbed a bit of old leaf. “Can’t stop,” he said. He mumbled because his mouth was full of leaf. “If I stop the whole place gets very untidy.”

He vanished underground, dragging the leaf with him.

"You see? It's just a matter of-keeping your eye and ears open," said a Ladybird who sat on a leaf about an inch from the Smallest Frog's nose. "You'll be surprised what you can find out if you try."

The vegetables and flowers all shook their leaves in agreement.

"It's not like my cave in the creek-bank," said the Smallest Frog.

"Of course it's not!" said the Ladybird. "This is a garden. Out there in the bush things can look after themselves very well unless people do something silly and upset them. But in this garden we all have to work extra hard because vegetables and flowers need extra help and have lots of enemies."

"Do you think you can fit in here, Little Frog?" asked Michael.

"Oh yes!" said the Smallest Frog in the World. "I like my cave in the creek-bank but it *is* a bit lonely for a little frog. I'd like to live here and help the vegetables and flowers grow properly. That is, if you'll have me."

"Of course we will!" said Michael, and all the listening creatures agreed. "You can have the old watering-can to live in. You'll need a sheltered spot on cold nights."

The Smallest Frog felt so happy! "My own private cave!" he shouted full of glee, "UK UK UK UK UK UK UK UK UK!"

Everyone laughed. But they laughed because they liked him.

So the Smallest Frog in the World joined the others in the garden and worked as hard as he could catching flies and unfriendly insects that tried to get in. All round him the creatures of the garden were busy doing their own jobs, and the Smallest Frog was very happy.

Michael put some water and some gravel and leaves into the watering-can. It was very comfortable to live in.

Sometimes on warm moonlit nights when he had finished his work in the garden the Smallest Frog would get into his watering-can cave and dream of the time when he was just a lonely little Spotted Grass Frog living on the creek-bank.

Then he would take a deeeeeeep breath and inflate his air sac and shout in his biggest voice: “UK UK UK UK UK UK UK UK!”

And because it sounded so loud as it echoed in the watering can all the creatures of the night would stop for a moment and listen.

UK!
UK! UK!

Published by New Holland Publishers
Young Reed an imprint of Reed New Holland Publishers

newhollandpublishers.com

First published by Lansdowne Publishing Pty Ltd 1980

ISBN: 9781921073953

A CiP record of this title is available from the National Library of Australia

Managing Director: Fiona Schultz
General Manager/Publisher: Olga Dementiev
Designer: Andrew Davies
Production Director: Arlene Gippert

Printed in China

Keep up with New Holland Publishers:
NewHollandPublishers
@newhollandpublishers